T0025882

YOUNG ZOOLOGIST
AFRICAN ELEPHANT

**A FIRST FIELD GUIDE TO THE
BIG-EARED GIANT OF THE SAVANNA**

CONTENTS

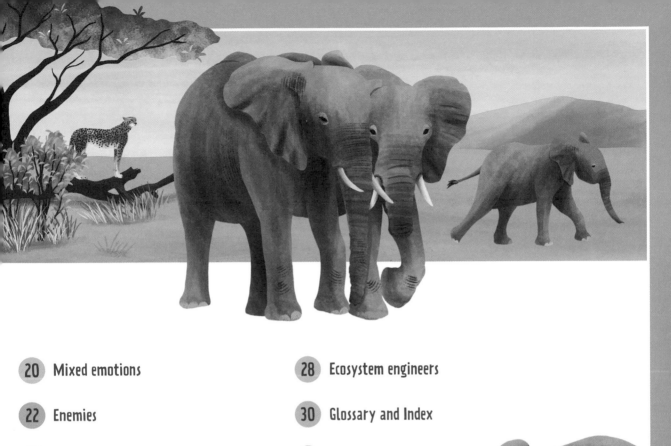

HELLO, YOUNG ZOOLOGIST!

My name is Festus W. Ihwagi and I grew up on the slopes of Mount Kenya in East Africa. The area I lived in was surrounded by thick forests that were home to lots of elephants! My parents were farmers, and every time potatoes and sweet corn were growing, elephants would come to feed on our crops at night. I was amazed at their size and beauty. When I grew up I studied zoology so I could learn more about elephants and other animals. Today, I work for a charity called Save the Elephants that protects these incredible creatures. I can't wait to tell you why I love African elephants!

DR. FESTUS W. IHWAGI

FACT FILE

SCIENTIFIC NAME
Loxodonta africana

TYPE
Mammal

FAMILY
Elephantidae

HEIGHT
Up to 10 ft (3.2 m)

WEIGHT
Up to 8,800 lb (4,000 kg)

HABITAT
Grasslands and forests

LOCATION
East, South, Central, and West Africa.

That's as much as four cars!

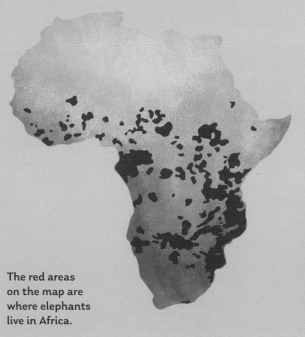

The red areas on the map are where elephants live in Africa.

EATS
Leaves, branches, roots, grasses, and fruit

LIFE SPAN
Up to 70 years

CONSERVATION STATUS
Endangered

BEFORE YOU GET STARTED

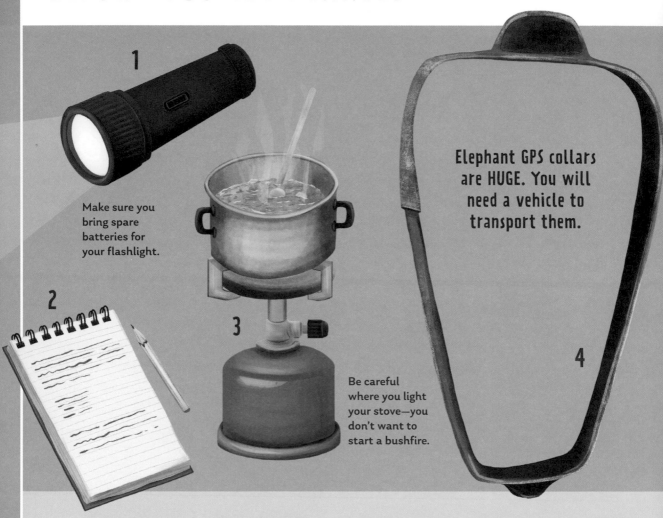

1 Make sure you bring spare batteries for your flashlight.

Elephant GPS collars are HUGE. You will need a vehicle to transport them.

2

3

Be careful where you light your stove—you don't want to start a bushfire.

4

1 **FLASHLIGHT**
A bright flashlight is essential. At night this will be your only form of light. There are many nocturnal animals to look out for—your safety depends on it.

2 **NOTEBOOK**
With so much to see and learn, a notebook and pen are crucial for zoologists. Write down all of the exciting things you see elephants doing.

3 **STOVE**
You'll do all of your cooking on a portable stove. Make sure that the stove has enough fuel before you set out. Otherwise you'll just be eating cold rations!

4 **GPS COLLAR**
You can hang a GPS (Global Positioning System) collar behind the ears of an elephant to monitor its location. It uses satellites in space to track the giants.

Elephants are usually found in the wilderness where no houses, electricity lines, or good roads exist. Before you set out to study elephants it's really important you're well prepared. Home is very far away!

5

Always zip up your tent when you leave it!

6

Insect repellent can save your life.

7

8

5 TENT
Always bring a tent that has enough space for all your belongings. Sleeping in a tent protects your food from monkeys and keeps the wind away at night.

6 INSECT REPELLENT
An insect spray is helpful to avoid insect bites at night. Mosquitoes and sandflies transmit many diseases, such as malaria.

7 TAPE MEASURE
Always have a tape measure on hand. You'll need it to measure various things you find, such as elephant teeth, bones, and footprints.

8 CAR
Walking in the wild areas where elephants live is incredibly dangerous. You'll need a car that can drive over rough, slippery, and wet surfaces.

MEET THE AFRICAN ELEPHANT

African elephants are the largest land animals to walk the Earth. They're famous for their huge ears, but the ears are not the only remarkable things about these giants. Let's take a closer look!

FLY SWATTER

An elephant's tail is about 4 ft (1.2 m) long. It has wirelike hairs at the tip and is used to swat flies away!

ANCIENT COUSINS

Mammoths are cousins of elephants that lived thousands of years ago. Mammoths were bigger than modern elephants and covered in shaggy hair.

SPONGY FEET

An elephant's foot is soft like a sponge to absorb shock and detect vibrations. Thick skin covers the foot to prevent injury.

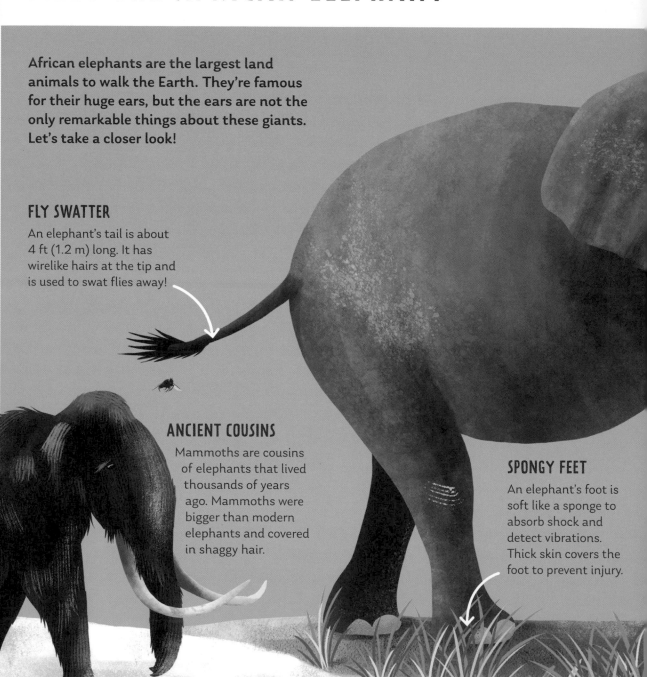

EYE SPY

Elephants don't have very good eyesight. They have long eyelashes to keep dust away.

BIG EARS

Elephants have lots of blood vessels in their giant ears. These help them cool down in the African heat.

OPEN WIDE

An elephant has 26 teeth. These include 12 molars, 12 premolars, and two incisors (tusks). Its tongue is enormous!

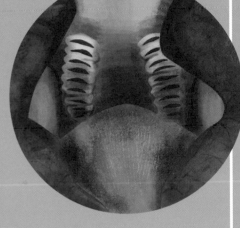

TUSKS

Tusks are giant incisor teeth. They grow throughout an elephant's life.

TRUNK

The trunk is a long nose full of strong muscles. It is used for trumpeting, drinking, smelling, and breathing.

NOSE TIP

An elephant can use its nose tip to pick up tiny objects like peanuts or sweet-corn kernels.

THE FAMILY

Savanna elephants
have the biggest ears.

Long, curved tusks

Smaller and
straighter tusks
make it easier
to walk through
thick bushes.

SAVANNA ELEPHANT

Savanna elephants are the
biggest and most widespread
species. Though they live mainly
in grasslands, they can also
be found in some forests.

There are two types of African elephant: savanna elephants and forest elephants. Another species of elephant lives in Asia. You can tell the difference between the three species by looking at their size and the shape of their tusks.

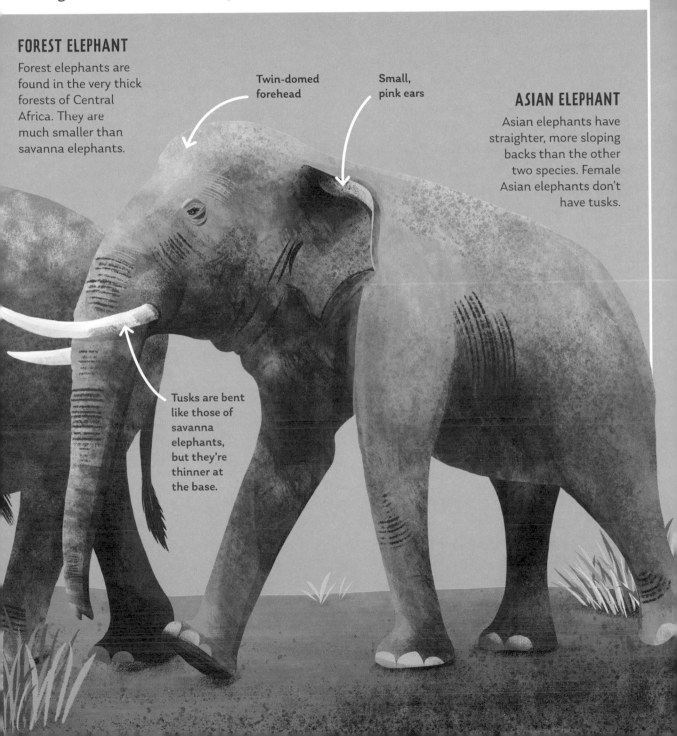

FOREST ELEPHANT

Forest elephants are found in the very thick forests of Central Africa. They are much smaller than savanna elephants.

Twin-domed forehead

Small, pink ears

ASIAN ELEPHANT

Asian elephants have straighter, more sloping backs than the other two species. Female Asian elephants don't have tusks.

Tusks are bent like those of savanna elephants, but they're thinner at the base.

FEMALE POWER

MATRIARCH

The matriarch is a bit like a grandmother in a human family. She is the oldest and largest female. The matriarch protects other members of the family and leads them to safe feeding areas.

MOTHERS

The mothers, often daughters of the matriarch, produce highly nutritious milk to help their calves grow quickly. The mothers take care of their calves for many years.

CALVES

Tiny calves are very playful. They can't see well at birth and locate their mothers by scent, sound, and touch.

Elephants like to stick together in herds. An elephant family is made up of an older female leader, called a matriarch, as well as several mothers, calves, and older siblings. Fathers stay alone, away from the herd, but visit various families from time to time.

An elephant family usually has between 3 and 25 members.

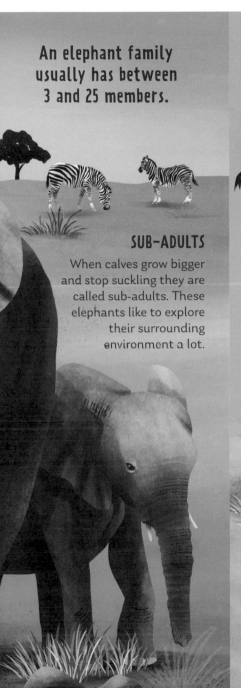

BABYSITTING

The sub-adult elephants help their mothers by babysitting the little ones. They make sure the small calves always walk between them to protect them from predators like lions. The sub-adults stay downstream of the calves when crossing rivers to stop them from being swept away by strong currents.

SUB-ADULTS

When calves grow bigger and stop suckling they are called sub-adults. These elephants like to explore their surrounding environment a lot.

FAMILY REFRESHMENTS

Elephant families drink together at least once a day. They can walk many miles in their search for water.

ELEPHANT CALVES

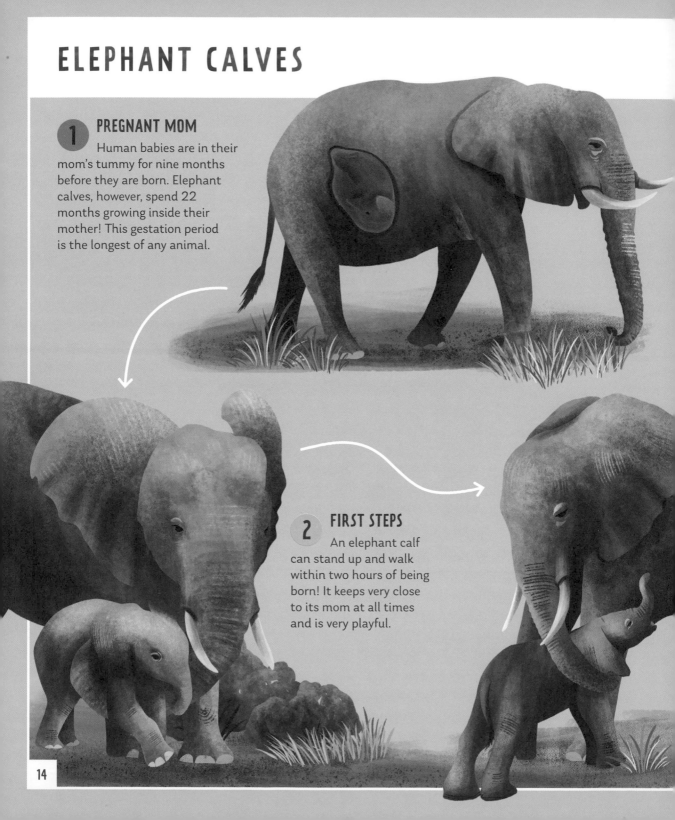

1 **PREGNANT MOM**
Human babies are in their mom's tummy for nine months before they are born. Elephant calves, however, spend 22 months growing inside their mother! This gestation period is the longest of any animal.

2 **FIRST STEPS**
An elephant calf can stand up and walk within two hours of being born! It keeps very close to its mom at all times and is very playful.

A young elephant is called a calf, just like a baby cow! Elephant calves look like mini adults, but their bodies are hairier. Life in the savanna is dangerous for the calves, so they rely on their mother and other members of the herd while they're growing up.

3 THIRSTY WORK
The calf begins to feed on leaves and grass at four months, but it continues to suckle milk for three years. It drinks water using its trunk and suckles with its mouth.

4 HERD PROTECTION
Members of the herd look after the calf. They protect it from predators and make sure it's safe when crossing dangerous rivers.

EATING AND DRINKING

EATS SHOOTS AND LEAVES

Elephants love the taste of fresh shoots from trees and shrubs. Using their trunks, they will reach up and grab the newest growth. Elephants will also often push trees down to reach the fresh shoots.

GRASS

Grass is easier to reach than fresh tree shoots. Using their trunks, elephants twist tufts of long grass to get a good grip and then pull hard to cut them.

Elephants eat for about 22 hours a day!

Elephants aren't picky eaters. They will happily eat food from lots of different species of plants. They'll snack on leaves, stems, bark, fruits, and even roots—whatever they happen to come across!

DRINKING

Elephants drink about 44 gallons (200 liters) of water a day, usually all at once!

Inside the tusks is a structure of woven lines. This makes them very strong and hard to break.

BARKING UP THE RIGHT TREE

It might not sound like a tasty snack to you, but elephants enjoy eating bark! They use their tusks to probe tree trunks and then strip off the bark with their trunks. It is very rich in nutrients.

TIME TO TALK

Elephants are very intelligent creatures and communicate with each other using their own sophisticated language. This language includes trumpeting, shaking their heads, and stamping their feet. When they're close to each other, elephants communicate by rubbing their bodies against each other or rumbling gently. Humans can hear some of the sounds they make, but not all of them.

Trumpeting can be heard from miles away!

TRUMPETING

Trumpeting is the most common form of elephant communication. An elephant makes these loud noises by squeezing air through their trunk. Trumpeting can be used to warn other members of the family that danger is nearby.

HEAD SHAKE

Head shaking is a way of intimidating other elephants or predators. An elephant will shake its big head from side to side, causing its ears to flap dramatically!

SEISMIC WAVES

Elephants produce vibrations called seismic waves that can only be detected by other elephants. They create these vibrations by stamping, and other elephants feel them through their feet. Seismic waves can travel farther than trumpeting.

Humans can detect seismic waves if they use a special listening device.

19

MIXED EMOTIONS

HAPPY

Happy elephants are very peaceful. They don't attack humans and are delightful to be around! Happy elephants don't hide from humans during the day, which makes them easier to study.

Happy moms stroke their calves and rumble softly.

Flapping ears gently is a sign of joy.

They like swinging their tail from side to side, kind of like dogs!

Elephants love coiling their trunks with each other.

Elephants can be exceptionally playful, especially when they visit the river to drink!

Never forget that elephants are wild animals. Even happy elephants can be dangerous.

Elephants are emotional animals. When studying them in the wild it's important to look for clues that tell you if they are happy or sad.

UNHAPPY

Unhappy elephants are extremely dangerous and shouldn't ever be approached. You can tell if an elephant is angry by looking at its posture. Unhappy elephants can charge at humans quickly and could easily kill someone.

An unhappy elephant throws dust up to warn that it's about to charge.

An anxious elephant has its tail stiffened and raised to one side.

An angry elephant will threaten an intruder by bashing bushes with its front legs and trunk.

ENEMIES

POACHING

Poachers kill elephants to get their ivory tusks. Poachers mainly hunt at night, when they can escape without being seen. Because of poachers elephant numbers in Africa have reduced dramatically. And it's not just the elephants that are killed that suffer—calves are left orphaned when their mothers are killed.

Poachers use guns to kill elephants.

Poachers targeting other animals for meat lay traps called snares. Elephants are often accidentally caught or injured by them.

UNWELCOME VISITORS

If elephants go near villages, the villagers will chase them away, often beating cooking pots to scare them.

Elephants are endangered animals. Their greatest enemies are humans. As more people build homes in the historical elephant ranges, conflicts occur. Hunters also kill elephants for their ivory tusks. This is illegal, but unfortunately it still happens frequently.

Ivory is prized by criminals because it is beautiful. Carvers make pieces of jewelry such as necklaces, earrings, and bangles using the tusks.

PREDATORS IN THE NIGHT

It's not just humans that elephants have to worry about. Lions hunt and eat small calves, especially at night. Elephants with calves avoid walking too much after dark to try to keep their calves safe.

LIVING ALONGSIDE ELEPHANTS

BEEHIVE FENCE

Believe it or not, elephants are scared of bees!
If a bee flies up an elephant's trunk, it can be very
uncomfortable. Because of this, zoologists advise
farmers to build fences with beehives in them to
keep elephants away.

The beehives are
covered with dry
grass and twigs
to keep them cool.

24

Elephants can be a bit of a nuisance for farmers who live alongside them. The giants like nothing more than to munch on fresh crops! Luckily zoologists have devised a system that keeps the farmers' crops safe while also not harming the elephants.

FLEE THE BEE!

The hives are linked with a wire. If an elephant touches the fence, the hives shake and bees come out buzzing. Elephants recognize the humming sound of angry bees and flee!

SWEET RESULT

An added bonus of the beehive fence is that it provides the farmers with honey. They can eat it and sell it along with their other crops.

ON THE MOVE

Most elephants travel large distances, or migrate, every year. When they see signs of rains in a far land, the matriarch will lead them off in search of fresh food. These journeys can last several days. Elephants also head off on these long journeys to visit their historic homes.

FOLLOW THE LEADER

The matriarch can remember the old routes to beautiful places she has visited before. She leads from the front, and the other elephants follow in a line.

RESTING IN THE FOREST

When elephants travel through dangerous areas inhabited by humans, they travel at night and hide in forests during the day to avoid being seen.

Elephants can walk nonstop for more than 37 miles (60 km) a day.

WILDEBEEST MIGRATION

While it's hard to predict when elephants will set off on their journeys, other species have more regular migrations. Wildebeest travel in great numbers with the changing of the seasons. They cross crocodile-infested rivers each year in search of good food and places where they can breed.

ECOSYSTEM ENGINEERS

THE POWER OF POOP

Elephant poop is called dung. Elephants poop eight to ten times a day! They walk long distances, and in the process they carry seeds of plants they have eaten from one place to another.

FOREST MANAGEMENT

When elephants push down trees, they open up the forest. Sunlight can reach the ground, and smaller plants can grow. Other animals come to the area to eat the young plants.

Fewer elephants in the wild is bad news for the other species that rely on them.

Elephants can completely change the ecosystems they live in. We call animals that do this ecosystem engineers. Other animals and plants depend on them—when elephants thrive, many other animals are happy too!

DIGGING FOR WATER

During the dry season, rivers and ponds dry up. Elephants dig holes in the soft riverbeds using their trunks to find underground water.

Smaller animals also use the elephant holes for a much needed drink.

DUNG BEETLE

Elephant dung is food for many beetles. Yum! Dung beetles make balls of fresh dung and roll them into their underground homes to store for later.

POOP PLANTS

When it rains, the seeds in the dung start turning into plants! The elephants have helped spread the plants across the ecosystem.

GLOSSARY

Calf
A young elephant or cow.

Dung
The poop of an animal like an elephant, cow, or buffalo.

Ecosystem
Plants and animals that live in the same habitat and interact with one another.

Endangered
Species are described as endangered when there are only a few individuals alive in the world.

Gestation period
The time it takes for a baby to grow in its mum's tummy.

Ivory
The white-colored material that forms the tusks of elephants and a few other animals.

Mammal
An animal that has warm blood and hair or fur, and nurses its young with milk.

Matriarch
The oldest elephant mother or grandmother in a family of elephants.

Migration
The movement of many animals at the same time from one place to another place that is far away.

Nocturnal
Describes animals that like to travel or eat at night.

Poacher
Someone who kills a wild animal without permission.

Predator
An animal that eats other animals.

Prey
An animal that other animals like to eat.

Snare
A trap for catching animals.

Sub-adult
An elephant that has stopped suckling but has not become a parent yet.

Trumpeting
Blowing out air through the trunk to produce a loud sound.

Trunk
The long nose of an elephant.

Tusk
The incisor tooth of an elephant.

Zoologist
A scientist who studies animals.

INDEX

31

This has been a

NEON 🦑 SQUID

production

To my daughters, Neema and Nataniah; son Ben-Gurion; and my wife, Margaret. I hope to inspire Neema, Ben, and Taniah to appreciate nature while they are still young.

Author: Dr. Festus W. Ihwagi
Illustrator: Nic Jones
US Editor: Allison Singer-Kushnir

Neon Squid would like to thank:

Jane Simmonds for proofreading.

Created for St. Martin's Press
by Neon Squid
The Stables, 4 Crinan Street,
London, N1 9XW

EU representative: Macmillan
Publishers Ireland Ltd,
1st Floor, The Liffey Trust Centre,
117–126 Sheriff Street Upper,
Dublin 1, D01 YC43

10 9 8 7 6 5 4 3 2 1

Library of Congress Cataloging-in-
Publication Data is available.

Printed and bound by Vivar
Printing in Malaysia.

ISBN: 978-1-684-49252-7

Printed in September 2022.

www.neonsquidbooks.com